Asymptotic American: Poems

Asymptotic American: Poems

Linda A.W. Brakel, M.D.

IPBOOKS.net
International Psychoanalytic Books

International Psychoanalytic Books
New York • http://www.IPBooks.net

Asymptotic American: Poems

Published by IPBooks, Queens, NY

IPBooks.net

Front cover layout by Kathy Kovacic, Blackthorn Studio
Interior design and layout by Noel S. Morado

ISBN: 978-1-956864-86-1

List of Poems

SECTION I: BROTHERS, MOTHERS, OTHERS

SECTION II: BIOLOGY

SECTION III: CONCEPTS

SECTION IV: BODY POLITIC

SECTION I: BROTHERS, MOTHERS, OTHERS

DOGGONE

Trigger the puppy
My first rejected writing project.
Teeth marks, red raw on Rob.
My puppy, my brother
Only brother
Only sibling.

Robert's slimy tears
My guffaws
Parents
Exiled Trigger.

Beagle or brother?
I'd take the dog.

Rob's biggest flaw, of many:
      (He'd say no fewer for me.)
He died, and stayed dead.

My brother needs a bigger poem.

LINDA A.W. BRAKEL, M.D.

FAMILY FOOTWARE
(My fashion statement tribute)

Today:
Left sock red   Right sock yellow
Tomorrow:
Left sock blue   Right sock red yellow

Uncle Ernie worked at a sock factory
Bonus pay:
Mismatched color outcasts.
He paired them,
Wore them,
Shared them with his younger brother,
My dad.

STILL IN THE CLOSET

3

Homosexuality	No more
Marital infidelity	No, never
Tax Cheat	No, nah

Uncle Kurt's academic papers,
My brother Rob's ashes,
Still in the closet
  With my orange ski jacket, striped wool hats, and assorted
mittens,
  With our volleyball net, baseball gloves and bats, tennis
rackets,
  With moth hole blankets, sleeping bags, and an old pup tent
Rob's ashes gather gloom and spiders
Amid
Dust castle webs.

  I don't miss brother
  I miss having a brother.

My brother warrants several poems.

LINDA A.W. BRAKEL, M.D.

DOUBLE AGENTS

During my pregnancy
I learned
First hand
Two-minded agency.

The cells grouping within me
Wanton wants:
Open jackets
Dark wet winds
Powdered donuts doused with orange juice
A canned tuna chaser.

Next, a sad sharp razor
An intimate alien agent eraser.

OPTIMISTS ABOUND

5

When we were young,
Childless and childish,
Bob and Amy feared
Their children might
Not come for Thanksgiving.

Now (30 years later) sometimes they don't.

We feared kids of ours
Would be born without
Heads.

We've spawned no kids,
Anencephalic or otherwise.
Our imaginary offspring
All have heads, fine heads.

LINDA A.W. BRAKEL, M.D.

AIRBAG DEATH

Buckled up, but
Killed by an Airbag.

Crampons on.
She lay flat on her face.
Caught in the ice
She worried she'd
Slide on.

He fell off his bike,
His stay-in-shape steed.
A massive concussion
He's forbidden to think,
Even to read.

Bats in their house
Bat bites?

Probabilities be damned
No hives,
No swelling of the face and throat,
No difficulty breathing,
No fast heartbeat, dizziness, or weakness.

"No," they said at County Health.
She got the shots (so did he).

Nobody died.

LINDA A.W. BRAKEL, M.D.

MY BROTHER WAS A TRAIN

My brother needs a bigger poem
He gets one here
But like the disappointing older sister
     I was
     And he knew
     When I was
     And when I wasn't
This poem will not be big enough.

****

So much music—folk, country & western, jazz, blues—
Is train music:
Movement, rhythm, change
     Leaving behind
     Starting afresh.

****

My father took the Long Island Rail Road
Every weekday
From Syosset to Jamaica to NYC.
Then back again.
My mother, brother, and I met him at the station.

****

Rob, fascinated and transfixed
Every day
"You want to be an engineer? Yes! Drive the trains?"
"No!" he'd say every day, "I want to be a train!"

****

My brother grew up a train.

****

Way before that, we rolled up together
    In his green rooster-patterned quilt
    Falling asleep together
    Falling from his bed together
    Falling outside parental view.
On a school night
    Our parents upset
    Seven years from her womb
    Five more than Rob
    World-savvy me
    Protection my job

****

After his girlfriend broke it off.
A college classmate
Threw himself on train tracks:
He lost the girl
And a leg.

****

A Swede walked onto Swiss tracks
Not a joke!
His suicide, measured, stately.

Rob didn't throw himself on train tracks
But he did walk slowly, imperceptibly, irrevocably into death.

Futile to stop a train.

My brother was a train.

NICETIES

We wrote them
At Mom's command.
     Dear Aunt Sadie,
     Thank you for the lovely $5 bills
You sent us for Hanukkah.
     Love, Linda & Rob
Rob dubbed her Aunt Sadist.
I laughed.

****

Bad handwriting,
Rumors to the contrary notwithstanding,
Is not a required Med School course.
I acquired bad handwriting all on my own.
I can't read it 5 minutes later.

****

Rob and I went to Padua.
As much as possible
We ate inky squid.

As much as possible
I practiced my talk.
He understood the science,
And translated my handwritten changes.
Rob saved that day.
Dear Aunt Sadie,
Dear Mommy,
Dear Rob,
Thank you
               Love, L

SIX WORDS

13

Not keen on rights for the unborn
　　Our abortion in 1993.
Not big on ceremonies after life ends
　　Siblings-and Parents-in-law cremated
　　　　　　Ashes dispersed
　　"Science Care" studied Rob's remains,
　　My brother's cremains remain
　　　　　　With us.
　　My Mother's ashes reside in
　　　　　　A military cemetery
　　　　　　Tribute to her life as wife
　　　　　　To my Father who served.

My father's ashes lie in Denver
　　　　　　I'm keen on an his stoney epitaph:

A Good Man, A Big Life

SMALL FOR MY SIZE

I'm small for my size
But I dream big.

I swing for the fences
But
I should
Bunt. I'm a
Sacrifice, Hit and Run, Steal a Base
Runt.

I should work on fine points,
Amass references galore.
Instead, I take on swaths,
Ignorance no block,
It's an open door.

Me, a team player?
Long longed for a team.
Turns out I'm a loner
Small and solo
I do what I can.

THERE *IS* SOMETHING LACKING

My Mother
Wanted a baby
So strongly
And then she got
Me.
My Mother
Wanted a child
So longingly
And then she got
Me.
My Mother
Wanted a girl
So explicitly—a girl
So that girl
Would love her
As she loved her
Mother,
But then she got me.

My Mother
Wanted a circle
Closed, close
Perfect
But then she got
Me.
I told myself

The heart of my imperfection
Lay in the imperfect
Circle of my heart's great vessels

But my Mother knew more.

"There is something lacking in you."
She said—
Not so much in anger,
As in truth.

SECOND OPINION
(Haiku on a Pediatric Cardiologist's Reference Group)
17

"You are so Lucky!"
Doc said. "My other patients
They'll soon be dead."

LINDA A.W. BRAKEL, M.D.

FUNNY, WHAT YOU REMEMBER

Uncle Ernie
>German Jew
>Drafted in America
>Fought in World War II
>Parachuter
>Captured
>Freed.

He remembered eating an orange:
>Victory
>Sweet
>Liquid
>Explosion
>Delight.

Uncle Ernie
>After the War
Studied Medicine
>Visited our family
>Often.
>Never
Remembered his toothbrush
His niece remembers:
>Delightfully Disruptive
>Finger toothbrush
>Loaded with toothpaste
>Gritty
>Sweet
>Wet.

Uncle Ernie
    Knew
    He could have been
    A concert pianist—

    If he played the piano.

****

He studied Medicine
At his graduation
    I was 5
    I got to stay up until 1am.

1955: all the Uncles, Aunts, and Cousins visited:
    Manfred & Margie
        Charlie & Rosie
    Kurt & Sarah
        Scott & Lucy
    Henry & Ruth
        Michael & Vivian
    Ernie
    Us (Walter, Paula + newborn, Rob) and me.
For the group photo
    All the cousins
    Wanted to be near Ernie.

    I won!
    My house!

1957: Uncle Ernie and Aunt Daphne
    Came to dinner twice a month.
    He
    Scraped the plates
    Gathered the glasses, the flatware, the bowls.
    Rolled up his sleeves.
    Water
    Hot
    Soapy
    Cascaded.

Uncle Ernie taught me
    Dish washing
    Is a doctor's job.

I always wash the dishes now—
    It's my house!

FRENCH SAVED MY LIFE

"French saved my life,"
My German Jewish father softly said.
"Why are you failing French?"

Born 1924: Itlingen, Germany
Fled 1936: Paris, France 1936-1940
Not a haven for Jews, but not a Hell.
He learned French and learned it well.
Rewarded with a ski trip to the French Alps.

In 1940:
Washington Heights, NYC
Drafted
Boot camp
Anzio
Italy, France, Germany
Recruited for the CIC—three crucial languages
German, French, and English
They saved his life.

But me?
I failed French, I did, and not just once.
But I too learned three other languages:
Frustration—no amount of toil could help my French.
Love—my father's love so sweet, intent on saving my life.
Sadness—"Dad" I said, quietly. "It won't be French"
             "Something else will have to save my life."

LEXIE THE LAST?

Rimsky was *my* first dog.
Eighteen pound feisty Lakeland Terrier
We went to College.
We lived in the country, he hung with the big dogs.
He knew the command "Come," answered "Maybe later."
If he saw prey or rivals through the backseat window,
He'd struggle to jump out in pursuit.

We went to Medical School.
He feared nothing other than thunder,
Found relief sitting on my head.
Rimsky, according to my classmate Karen,
Preferred NYC to our Boston school.

We went to Residency in Ann Arbor.
A shrink asked, "What does your dog do, when you are away all day working?"
"I don't know, I'm away all day working."
Rimsky allowed select men into our lives,
Including (luckily) my husband.

Rimsky died five years later, a terrier for 18.5 years,
Almost to the end.

Jet Ann was *our* first dog.
"Active and Quiet" her label read at the Pound.
We rescued her
She saved us.
Black and sleek. A down-sized German Shepard/Coyote
Who jumped on the kitchen table her first day home,
Who would never go into our basement,
Who bristled at children,
Who caught tennis balls before they bounced,
Who'd run ahead on trails, but check back on us, concerned.
Active, exuberant until age 17.
We spent her last day holding her, quiet.

Xenia as a puppy ate her bed(s).
Beautiful, Greyhound-Whippet Lurcher Rescue Dog.
Stately, graceful. Fast!
Barely passed dog school, but we won the Quick Sit Contest.
Feared people, loved dogs.
Dog school people were ok, *they* had dogs.

We dealt with her and
With my aging parents.
Would they resent our divided care?
But surprise!
They loved Xenia, and she them.
When Xenia died at 15, her grand-people were
Already
Buried.

Lexie is a playful protean sprightly mite,
Black with 2 white paws, one eye blue, the other yellow,
30 pounds of love, the website claimed.
12 breeds in her origin story.
Leaps great heights, and over sofa backs,
Kills two small mammals per month.
An escape artist—we put up new fences just for her.

Lexie zooms!
But this question looms:
Will Lexie be *our* last dog?

How long will *our* last?

AORTA SONG

Summer 1970
Aortic Aneurysm.

O, I don't want to be sick
O, I don't want to be ill.

Summer 2024
Cardiologists follow me, but
Not on X,
Not on Academia.edu,
Not on Research Gate—
On scans and probes.

Aorta no bigger
Stable
I own
It.

Karen has hypertension, Mike, kidney disease, Art, bronchiectasis and
a DVT, Spider, tricky knees, Denny, diabetes—type 1, autoimmune.
They're 65+ Covid's way worse than flu. Susy has bad hips replaced,
Dennis and Mickey, too (six hips—hooray?), Barb, fibromyalgia,
Arthur, PMR. Crick and Jim have had Myocardial Infarctions, Chris
survived two cancer bouts, Ivan, TIAs, Larry and Judie, demented, Ira
on his way? Dick spent 10 years on dialysis, died the other day.
I used to think…sometimes still do

When my reference group had me AND you,
I'd feel better.
Not True.

Linda A. Orta now sings a different song:

O, I don't want to be sick
O, I don't want to be ill

At 72—I accept, I do
The universe will do with me
Exactly what it will.

Next Scan: December
 I shan't die young.

SHOOTING STAR

I shan't die young
And my husband, my love,
Older than I
Has yet to die.

The first time we met   I set up our wedding   Only my people
The next time we met   We refrained   We desired
The 7th time we met   (Maybe 6th or 8th)   We got it on!

43 years hence
Uncountable times.
No scented candles,
Nor soft lights,
Nor Fireworks,
We're not Rocket types
Simple day-to-day, body-to-body
Elegance.
Spare we are
But not spare with care.

We had our first date, first fight, first sleep over, first trip,
first day living together, first big fight, first job scare, first health scare,
first friends' divorce, first pregnancy, first abortion, first dog together,
first bird, first pet's death, first friend's death, first parent's death, first
sibling's death
Rinse and Repeat

What about the last?
Even the penultimate?

My husband is 81.
Today he ejaculated—
Shooting star!

Will this be the last time?
What would I do if I knew?

Nothing Different.

NOTHING, MAYBE NOTHING

(Following, with gratitude, from "Punctuation" by Clint Smith)

"I apologized for nothing."
>He meant either:
>>a) Circumstances reveal there was no need for the apology he just offered her.
>>b) There was never a circumstance in which he meaningfully apologized to her.

"You may be right."
>She meant either:
>>a) He could be right.
>>b) More likely, he's wrong.

She said, discussing the MRI of his head: "They found nothing."
>She meant either:
>>a) They discovered no pathology.
>>b) They found no brain at all.

Scenes from a long marriage:
Maybe it was OK,
More likely, not.

RHYTHM & BLUES

I
Heart Defect, Heat Failure, Heart Broken, Heart Sick.
Heart Imaged, Heart Working, Heart Surgery, Heart Fixed.

II
Heart Works
Heart Strong.
But
Heart Wrong
Head Strong.
Normal Heart Longed for
All along
"One normal heart, please."

III
Trade?
Normal, Just Average Body/Life
For Average Heart—No Strife
No Cardiologists
I've worn out six
This wish, Quixotic

IV
Warm Heart, Brave Heart, Bold Heart
Fine
Dear Heart, True Heart,
Heart of Mine

REQUIEM FOR TEX (2005-2023)
(Resourceful Hunter, Trusty Pack Member)

Change is subtle
Change is swift
Change is in the air
Change is in the soil
My friend,
Change is everywhere.

Try to stop it
You cannot
Try to just hang on.

You can't change what you can't see
You can't change what's not foreseen
You can't change what you can see
You can't change what's in between.

You can't change the slow erosion.
You can't change the sharp explosion.

Plants will wither, some still flower
Rain will shower.
Fiends grab power, critics glower.
Dogs still die.
Dogs will die.

Young ones flourish
Not discouraged
Takes some courage
To be born, to grow.

To end a life
Will bring new sorrow
Will end some sorrow
Maybe tomorrow.

Not Today.

POEM FOR FOUR
(After Aracelis Girmay's "Ode to Letter B")

Four's my number
Since I was 4
I wanted to be 44

I couldn't imagine 4444,
But at 4, I
Didn't do math.

Our car had 4 doors,
My father had 4 Brothers,
Baseball had (has) 4 Bases,
I had (almost) 4 friends,
Our fourth family member
Was underway.

My amour for Four spread to "for" and "fore"
Better to be for something than against
Good to have forethought—
Prevents careening through the fence.

Arguments with 4 sides,
Better than two?
Animals with 4 legs,
Strides more fluid, true.

****

What would we be without four, both number and word?

****

We wouldn't sweat Colombus Day, no 1_92.
We wouldn't need the leap year fix every _ years.
No one would crazy-chant at Donald Trump, _more years!
Would our democracy be safe?

Golfers would not be safe at all.

Without the Roman 4 (not five)
The world would be without I.V.s
Many no longer alive.

****

When I was 4 and hunting 4-leaf clovers—
My Dad and I made do
With abundant clovers wearing three,
Not two.

MUSINGS ON LEASHES (LEASHES ON LIFE)

(Inspired by Mary Oliver's "The Summer Beach")

The poet has said
That a dog who
Walks leashed all its life, obedient
"…--is what a chair is to a tree."

Agree!
And yet
Unleashed, untethered
I have been
No better off.
Unhinged thus
Then when, I, by the way,
Not a dog
Have been leashed and tethered.

Dogs I've lived with (never long enough)
Loved as deep as I go
Some unleashed   Sometimes
All leashed   Sometimes
None obedient
They tell me:

"I want to be with you"
Or "I don't."
"I want to go faster."

"I want to go slower."
"I want to stop to smell
      Everything—an oak tree twig, those 3-leaf clovers, that clump
         of dirt, the butt of a cig
      Anything—a chocolate bar wrapper, that blade of grass,
         Roxie's nose and her ass
      All that I know and knew
      All that is now new.
"I want to pee:
      Here—on that maple tree truck
      There—at the Argus Building corner, on the "For Rent"
         wooden stake
      There—where I pooed yesterday, on that yellow flower
      There—2 feet from where you saw raccoons years ago, and I
         saw a squirrel tomorrow
      Here—at our garbage can."
"I want to greet/smell that dog.
      No, not *that* one,
      Yes, the one across the street, smiling at me."
"I don't want to go home, yet. . .
 I'm happy to be home"

"Please pick up the leash soon
      Before the next full moon
      Before tomorrow's noon.
"I love its smell, its noise, its look."
"It says a walk is coming soon."

HOW TO TIE YOUR SHOES

My brother requires a bigger poem
He does.
I try. But so far I've failed.

A Smaller poem
Allows, Promotes
A Quieter inner wail.

****

Whenever I have mechanical trouble
Rob, boy brother
Comes to mind, as
Dad was not the "fix-it" kind.

Gilbert's disease:
A good and lucky mutation
Staves off old age ruination.
But for Rob, there was no staving
He had many early old age ails,
The worst: Parkinson's flails.
Often as I mistype a letter, screw up a password, or I.D.
I think of my brother: if I were he
How much worse would I be?

Looking back, he did poorly,
We did poorly too.
But one connection he thought through
A You-Tube: "How to tie your shoes."
I saw Rob learn the task at 5
Then, at 64, soon not alive
Why?
Why play this You-Tube
For his older, sadder sister?

SECTION II: BIOLOGY

FLY ON THE WALL

My bedroom walls
Want hearing aids.
The walls in my bedroom
Have flies.
The flies on the walls
Want compound glasses
To fit their compound eyes.

What are they looking for?
What will they hear?
A secretive cyclonic roar? A
Passionate magical mystery tour?

Flies on the walls:
Find out.
Then tell *me*!

LINDA A.W. BRAKEL, M.D.

EOSINOPHIL

42

White cells, red dye, blue bloods
    More
Sick cell, sickle cell, cell mates
    Floors
        Pediatrics
        Orthopedics
        Heme-onc
        G.Y.N.
        Surgery
        Emergency
        I.C.U.
I.C.U.
But do I really?

    ****

Eosin dye
And yes!
We all will.
No joy in this
No love. No phil-.

X,Y,Z

43

Levaquin's real name is Levofloxocin,
Losartan is Cozaar to her friends.

Infliximab (Remicade) is related to adalimumab (Humira),
Cousins both to Rinvoq (Upadacitinib) by the way.

Sildenafil is generic for Viagra.
Cialis lasts half a week.
Call it its generic, tadalafil.
You'll seem smart
With erections on demand.

Prozac, Paxil, Zoloft for depression
Ozembic, Rybelsus lower A1c.

Would that drug naming
Were left only to me.

Abilify: Psychosis-Gone Now
Zestril: Blood Pressure Low
No Zs, Qs, Vs, and Xs,
Keep the Ks for Skrabble
Down with corporate drug name psycho-babble.

LINDA A.W. BRAKEL, M.D.

COVID/CORVID

COVID
Rhymes
Imperfectly with
Katydid
And
Perfectly with
PaxlOvid

But
Lo!
Pax-LO-vid
has vid to VID
And LO to CO

HO
And it prevents
Death too

****

COVID 19
Corvid 19
4 and 20 black crows
Minus 5
In rows
19 Crows
Ravens raving
Ravens singing

****

COVID
Morbid
Pax-LO-vid
Corvid

In birds we trust.

THINKING MORE NOW
ENJOYING IT LESS

I used to think
I don't
Anymore?
     But
COVID
     Compels
     Cognition
     Constantly
     Cogitating
     Concerning
Anything
Everything
Every Little Thing
Including
Entailing:
     Should I go:
     To the store?
     To the tavern?
     To your house?

     Should I wear a mask?
     Will you?
     Should I test?
     Will you test too?

One day
Two days
Three days
More?
Am I just
A rhyming bore?

Is this visit a risk?
No visit a risk too?
One, two
What's one to do?

COVID
    No in between
    Flexible bending
    Feels akin
    To surrender.

I used to think
Now I think more.

LINDA A.W. BRAKEL, M.D.

BAT AND VIRUS: 4 HAIKUS, PLUS A QUESTION POEM (<u>VIRUS</u>)

WERE I A BAT
   (With appreciation for Thomas Nagel's "What it's like to be a bat")

Were I a bat, would
I be I? Jagged Night Flight
Slicing through Night Sky.

WERE I A VIRUS
Were I a virus,
I'd be at home in a bat
In sync, we'd like that.

BATS AND VIRUSES: EVALUATIONS
That bat, *that* virus
I'd be grateful for the help—
Best rating on YELP

OUR BAT-SHARE HOUSE
Imminent flight risk
Bat in *our* house, in a wall
Black-caped danger, small

VIRUS?
Virus!
Are you alive?

ODES TO THE BODY: 5 HAIKUS, PLUS A STATEMENT POEM (<u>T.O.D.</u>)

SONG OF THE HEART
Heart beats, heart beats, heart
Beats on, cantors and gallops
Until life is gone.

CLOSE TO THE BREAST
Right breast then Left Breast
Time for my yearly screening,
My inner screaming.

EYE (I) SEE
Cloudy fovea
In your eye exam today
Must sharp vision fray?

GUT CHECK
Food good. Eating well.
Yet for me at 73
Colonoscopy.

BRAIN CHECK
Your flaws are hidden,
Except for the ones that show.
Do dark tangles grow?

TIME OF DEATH
A Time of Death (TOD) is everyone's fate.
Yet, don't be early just to be late.

FLOWER DIRGE

51

Lovers never brought flowers.
No bad feelings bloomed.
Pretty though flowers can be,
Cut, they're dead.

A dirge a day
To purge the wilted
From the spray

Cleaved from the rest
They've failed life's test.

SECTION III: CONCEPTS

PERDURANCE

55

Dust gathers
Wipe it away

It
Comes back
As
Dust

Neither created
Nor destroyed

Dust
Perdures
Re-arranged

LINDA A.W. BRAKEL, M.D.

ASYMPTOTIC AMERICAN

Germans seek perfection,
Americans prefer to strive.
Always improve,
Never arrive.

Asymptotic American,
That's me!
The end of "The American Century"
Disrupts, chafes, burns, wounds.

What about me?
"Improve" after seventy?
Understand more?
Tolerate more?
Maybe. Probably not.

Friends become non-friends.
Friends and family die.

And my body…?

Old age perfection?
I'm no German
I'll take the asymptote.

I WANT THEREFORE I AM

57

If you don't have what you want
And don't want what you have,
You are wanting.

If you don't have what you want
And want what you don't have,
You are wanting.

If you have what you don't want
And don't want what you have,
You are wanting.

If you have what you want
And want what you have…

Throw you a fish!

LINDA A.W. BRAKEL, M.D.

BRAIN-IN-A-VAT LACKS BODY FAT

A Brain-in-a-Vat lacks body fat,
But he worries nonetheless.

Mary, famed color scientist, is color-blind,
But she can explain
The colors she can't see.

A Zombie I know *seemed* quite excited, singing a colorful song,
But with secret *shame* he sang to me,
But no feelings came along.
And not just when he sings his songs,
He *admits* he feels nothing at all.

My head is bursting,
I'm seeing red,
I'm seething, blaring with rage.
If I were a brain-in-a-vat,
Could I burst out?
Or would I end up
A sad, sad brain-in-a-cage?

One thing for sure
I feel too much! A Zombie I am not!
But my Zombie pal claims just the same—
He's *distrawsed, angry, hot.*

"Mirror neurons be damned,"
We both exclaim at once:
Too complex this philosophical knot:

Let's do lunch.

LINDA A.W. BRAKEL, M.D.

ARE YOU ALIVE?: LAST LINE COMPENDIUM FROM SELECTED POEMS

Addressed to viruses everywhere

Are you alive?   (Virus)

I don't   Know   (Ghost Poem)
Sad   (A Day in January)

[Let's invent] An intimate alien agent eraser   (Double Agents)
[Would you be] Immune to such affronts?   (Ghost Poem)
[But, could we] Disturb your DNA/RNA?   (Ghost Poem)
[Have it] Re-arranged   (Dust)

[COVID-19: To you I say] Not all lives [you take] are counted
                                                           (Real Numbers...)
[To Zika: May those infected be born] All with fine heads
                                                           (Optimists Abound)

FIRST POETRY CLASS

61

Haiku, we love you!
Villanelle, go straight to Hell.
Sonnet, we're on it.

LINDA A.W. BRAKEL, M.D.

SPELLCHECK, CHATGPT, AND ME

Spellcheck oversees:
Over-writing my writing.
Making right my writing?
As the driver's ed instructor
Over-drove my driving.

"Oh the driver's dead,"
Said Spellcheck and ChatGPT together.
"We're sad for you."

****

Something's dead or dying
In the USA—
USA Today.

DeSantis veers to Trump's right.
Trump could run again and win.

****

"Turn your steering wheel right and quick."
Yelled the driver's ed teacher, growing sick.

"The driver who is dead is a teacher,"
Said Spellcheck and ChatGPT, elated:
"We figured it out."

I wanted to steer left.
Go left young woman,
Go left!
And so I have.

I taught my Brooklyn friend to drive
In Boston
On Rotaries.
She'd only turn right
Especially at night.
Go left young woman.
She went
Left.

****

ChatGPT and Spellcheck now somber, intoned:
"Oh, you are the driving teacher who died.
Our condolences to you about you."

"Does that even make sense?"
I asked them, pissed at their illogic.
"We sense urine," they said.
"Is there some trouble you're in?"

Probably yes,
But I've not yet died.
Yet there's a stench:
And just like the French,
We must protest

The unfair air.
It's everywhere.
So hard to start,
No helpful chart.

"A pointer could help,"
Said the ever-helpful ChatGPT.
"German long-haired or short
Either likely to get to the root."
"I totally, 100% agree,"
Asserted our Spellcheck
Assented by me—
We three sing-songing
Merrily.

FLOW CHART

65

Tooth & Nail / Nail & Tooth
Hearty & Hale/Lies & Truth
Fish or Fowl
Succeed or Fail

Success so sweet
Too often
    Fleet
Try Try   Accept
Again   Defeat

Fail Safe
Failure to Thrive
    Dead or Alive
    Dead Survive
Dead Revive

LINDA A.W. BRAKEL, M.D.

EPIPHENOMENAL OR NOT

Epiphenomenal or not:
Consciousness?
Is
All we've got.

ESOTERIC RIDDLE

67

The star of this riddle
Appears
When we discuss
You, me, and her
Him, her, and them
Me, myself, and I.

Yet the star disappears
When we consider
You, me and her
Him, her and them
Me, myself and I.

The answer to the riddle
Is not in
Pronouns: female, male and non-binary
Nor in
Self, other and questions of identity.

But the riddle twinkles
As we take up
Pronouns: female, male, and non-binary
Self, other, and questions of identity.

What gives?
A paradox?
But wait, don't jump out of your sexy sox.

It's too much drama
For
The famous, one, and only

Oxford Comma!

COFFEE AND TEA

Art, a linguist, and Dennis, a physicist
Concluded, after 50 years of coffees—
There's no free lunch.

Karen, a pediatrician, and Lindsay, a psychiatrist
Concluded, after 50 years of teas, that
Nothing's perfect.

No thing, event, or process
Can be perfect.
Only nothing
Is perfect.

No moving parts
Zero—0—no snags, no kluges, no excess, no lack,
No need for redundance or work-arounds,
Flawless circle, Round.

If the Perfect is the enemy of the good,
And Nothing is Perfect,
The Good, clearly better than Nothing,
Is also better than Perfect.

Oooooff!
Re: the above proof.
But
Let's agree:
Lunch,
Neither free nor perfect,
Is a better deal than dinner.

SPOT ON

X marks the Spot.

I met my hero, Spot
In the first-grade reader.
Run, Spot run.
See Spot run.
Hear Spot speak.
Speak Spot speak:

I am a versatile spot,
And I'm best

On dogs:
Dalmatians, English Pointers, German Long-Haired & Short-Haired
Pointers, Springer Spaniels, English Setters, Australian Cattle Dogs,
Australian Shepherds, Great Danes, Bluetick Coon Hounds, Border
Collies, Brittany Spaniels, Catahoula Leopard Dogs, Jack Russell
Terriers, Wirehaired Pointing Griffins, Corgis, Mixed Breeds, even
Dingoes, African Wild Dogs, and Hyenas.

I'm Okay on:
Big cats, other mammals, birds, reptiles, amphibians, fish, even insects
profit from my presence: Leopards, Cheetahs, Jaguars, Giraffes,
Horses, Pigs, Deer, Mice, Spotted Owls, Starling yearlings, Frogs,
Lizards, Snakes, Trout, Lady Bugs, and Japanese Beetles.

I'm a trouble-maker on:
Shirts and ties, jackets, skirts and dresses, spots on rugs and carpets.

I'm known for:
Spotty attendance, spotty audiences, spotty work.

Worse yet, I'm responsible for:
Spots on lungs, Spots on Skin, Spots in Bone, Spots on X-rays/
MRI/ CT scans, gangrenous spots, Rocky Mountain Spotted Fever,
Malignant Spots.
Dark Spots
Dead Spots.

If I were British, now would be the time to offer

A Spot of Tea
A Safe Spot

I work sometimes on:
Soft Spots
Spots on Radio and TV shows
Spot Checks

Best of all,
I'm
A
Hot Spot
Sun Spot
Spot in the Sun
In the Spotlight

SPOT ON

Spot Remover
Run, Spot, Run!

LINDA A.W. BRAKEL, M.D.

ON NOT KNOWING—A SONNET

I (not) know in a cloud, cumulous cloudy.
I (not) know as a vector, opposing rays.
Sometimes insight arrives jagged, rowdy.
Sometimes insight springs at once, shines, displays.

I (not) know things I ought—Am I no one's dolt?
I (not) know matters I've been taught.
Sometimes answers come fast: lightning bolt.
Sometimes answers come slow and frought.

My sphere of knowledge, just tangential,
My knowledge globe, whole, not a fraction.
Someday my thinking might prove consequential,
No expectation that my work will find traction.

I do know what I know, less what I know not,
But what I (not) know, still seems a lot!

SECTION IV: BODY POLITIC

A DAY IN JANUARY

Half-mast,
Our flag:
20 shot
Half men, half women,
Half dead
Asian on Asian.

Lunar New Year
Year of the Rabbit—
No Rabbit's Foot
In San Bernardino.

It's not right, but half the country is…
Maga Right

Killer was 72.
What was he doing half a life ago?
36 mass shootings this January.

It's winter, cold
People walk
To work,
To school with kids.
Half have dogs on leashes,
All have phones on leashes—
Short leashes.

LINDA A.W. BRAKEL, M.D.

IT COULD HAVE BEEN DIFFERENT

I could have been born a boy,
I could have been born in June,
If the year were 3016,
I could have been born on the moon.

I could have been born a Moor,
I could have been born on shore,
If I had been born a mongrel pup,
I'd likely be one of four.

I am a mongrel girl.
I could have been born down South.
If I had been born in the South,
Would I have had a silver spoon
Or a Confederate flag in my mouth?

I could have been born with no wealth,
I could have been born lacking health,
If I had been born black as onyx,
Would that require secret stealth?

As it is   I was born   My Self
Not black
Not blue
A girl
A Jew

No Reason
Un Just Rhyme

REAL NUMBERS THAT ARE NEVERTHELESS HARD TO IMAGINE

79

Questions: How many "regular" people died the day JFK was shot?

How many "regulars" died as a direct result?

Answers: Lee Harvey Oswald = One

If Lee Harvey Oswald was a "regular",

The answer is: 1 + Hard to Imagine = ?

If Lee Harvey Oswald was not a "regular" person,

The answer is Hard to Imagine.

Conclusion: All lives count?

Not all lives get counted.

LINDA A.W. BRAKEL, M.D.

LESSONS FROM MY HAMMER TOE

Hammer Toes can hurt.
But
Not so much as wars.

Today's high at 2pm: 18°
Fahrenheit.
No water, heat,
No lights.
Two days of this
For first-world us.
Did I empathize?

No, just
An insight spark:
My Guppy
Inconvenience
vs.
Blacks'
Real Grievance
Shark.

Yet when
My Hammer Toe hurts,
Hard to give a hoot
About severe pain
In another's foot.

BODY POLITIC-1

81

They say: We are the richest nation ever known. We are the only country founded on an idea. We are the land of the free, home of the brave

So why:

So many homeless? Great inequality? Poor education? No reparations for enslaved peoples' descendants? Systemic racism? Too few immigration lawyers and judges? Insufficient IRS tools to catch fat cat tax cheats?

And for Christ's sakes why don't we tax wealth?

How can we allow: Slow or no coming to Justice for the well-connected unrepentant? Yet speedy and harsh (in)justice to punish the unconnected? Unheeded majority desires on abortion, guns, wages, healthcare?

Democracy to be thwarted without recourse to repair?

****

Aspirational America flows, floods, flames away.
Slowly with each Confederate flag flying and not at half-staff
Quickly with re-ignited "lost causes."

****

After this unpoetic rant you *should* ask me: Do you love America?

Do I love my arm?

Do I love my leg?

Do I love my knees and hips?

Do I love my spleen?

Do I love my finger tips?

Or only when they hurt?

Do I love my neurons—axon, body, dendrites, all?

Do I love my cells' ribosomes?

And their vacuoles for dirt?

My body is my home

In sickness and in health,

My body lives here

In poverty and wealth,

Do I love America?

What's love got to do with it?

THE REIGN OF ANTS

Vivid colors bring joy, but
Also harm.
The yellow "*Jude*" and the red Nazi armbands
Left World War Two with my soldier father,
And
Found a home in my parents' bedroom,
In a grey dusty drawer, rarely opened, musty.

****

Charlottesville 2017
"Jews will not replace us."
Tiki torches blazing, screeching orange flames:
"Jews will not replace us."
Scorched collective American conscience:
"Jews will not replace us."

Our orange tufted leader:
"Very fine people on both sides."
"Jews will not replace us."

All this in America as
Cousin Sam,
Kindertransported to England
At 14.
At 94, honored for Holocaust teachings.
by Queen Elizabeth II,

Who earlier, but in the same royal colors,
Celebrated UK colonialism.

****

Back in the USA
Beautiful, but dutiful, German Shepards dogs
With police, python hoses
Torment torrents,
Black integrators young and old.

America,
Why is our landscape
Sprinkled with Lost Cause paraphernalia?
Worse, Confederate flags?

Is this flag a native flower? (No, it's a weed.)
But Black people live here!

Would cousin Sam move to Himmler Strasse?
Would you dwell among swastikas?

Braxton Bragg,
Jubal Early,
George Pickett,
P.G.T. Beauregard,
Bloody Bill Anderson,
Stonewall Jackson,
James Longstreet,
Robert E. Lee.

Confederate "heroes"?
American streets?

Statues
Atop grand graceful horses of bay, black, and grey
Bestride the world of green, lush, public parks
For everyone to see, including
Black people who live here!

Eradicate the riders and keep the magnificent horses

****

"Jews will not replace us."
No, Jews try to replace slaughtered Jews.
Migrants will replace you.
Ants too.

Ants outnumber humans 2.5 million to one.
Their Queens will replace you.
You'll find this OK.
They are American ants,
And
Ant colonies brook no genetic diversity.
But do remember:

Mostly they are black.

BODY POLITIC-2

Living here in the USA
I've done some good,
Made some friends and too much money,
But my outlook's hardly sunny.

1.

As all the king's horses
And all the king's men
(And my paltry fortune)
Won't put the country together again.

2.

Regardless of wealth,
The body degrades,
But among the lucky
Degrading proceeds
With implacable stealth.

****

I've sung my home team's anthem:
The helpless agents' song, in two verses.

DOUBLE SONNET:
COVID-19 AT YEAR THREE

Yeah, it's year three, so
No more lockdowns
Quarantines
Mandates.

Most Americans will be OK, or so we think—
Except if you're old, infirm, immune weak.
Well, you do have FREEDOM. You
Control your fate.

Hell, buy a gun, an AR-15,
Vent your green spleen with the lovely machine.
You can carry it proudly concealed, maybe open.
It won't kill viruses but it works well on people.

You can't plan a family: Abortion's restricted.
Great: Add kids 7 and 8; you're no longer conflicted.

****

FREEDOM!
I digress
So now back to COVID
With less distress.

The odds of bad COVID
Are not all that poor.
And final great news:
If you're over 64

How long
Will you live,
COVID
Or not

Given the years
You've already shot?

MOSTLY THEY ARE BLACK

Mostly they're black
Absorbing heat,
No light back.

Red splotches on wings,
Songs laced with meaning,
Songs redwing blackbirds sing.

Not riffs of jazz, not just like the blues,
They're more akin to chants of Jews.

****

Mostly they're Black
Absorb history's heat
No light back.

Red splotches: raw wounds and toil
Inside lungs, and guts, and bone, or
Outside working American soil.

Songs twined with meaning,
Songs meant to sing.
Sweet songs, pained songs,
Jazz, and blues
Different from hypnotic chants of Jews.

Clear and loud,
Black and proud
Joyous music, exuberant
Release from white folks' bonds.

****

Why would anyone find it better to be White?
Why would anyone feel outrage, feign fright?

To take aim at Black flights of delight
Like marksmen, disturbed and absurd,
Shooting, maiming, killing black birds?

BIGLY

An incomplete list
Not to insist
It might help quell
If not yet dispel
The fury and outrage
In our USA hell.

John F. Kennedy (#35) in Berlin,
Solidarity with Berliners
Asserted:
"Ich bin ein Berliner!"
He meant: "I'm from Berlin!"
He said: "I'm a Jelly donut."

A popular pre-election slogan for (#37):
"Why change dicks in the middle of a screw?"
"Vote for Dick Nixon '72!"

Jimmy Carter (#39):
Famously lusted in his heart.
(Bless his truth-telling heart—
He called Israel's apartheid
APARTHEID!)

Side note: After a report on Carter's inner lust,
A news channel featured a live meeting:
Diplomats—US and the USSR—convened at a table

The chyron below, out of sync (or maybe prescient),
Read:
"Beware, these men are pickpockets."

Interviewer: "Why do you want Carter's job?"
Reagan (#40): "I don't want Jimmy Carter's job; I want to be
President."
And as President he helped those not-well-off to become
Less-well-off.

George H.W. Bush (#41):
On an eco-friendly proposal
Protested: "We'll be up to our neck in owls!"
Later against Clinton/Gore:
"My dog, Milly, knows more about foreign policy than those two
Bozos!"
Wise Milly!

Let's "thank" H.W. for
Clarence Thomas, William Barr, and John Roberts.

In 1998, Clinton (#42) "defended" himself stating:
"It depends on what the meaning of 'is' is."
I wonder if he's figured it out?

George W. Bush (#43):
"I'm the decider."
Enough said. Lives lost.

About Barack H. Obama (#44):
Bumper Sticker: "If you can't vote for Obama because he's black,
Vote for him because he's white."

Sarah Palin, unworthy running mate of the defeated John McCain
Zinged Obama:
"How's that hopey-changey thing working for you?"

Donald J. Trump (#45) claimed that
Were he to shoot someone on 5th Avenue,
He'd not lose a single vote.
Sadly, he'd likely get a lot more.

He prescribed:
Bleach and inner light
To cure the "China flu."

A million died
On Trump's watch,
(Many) Needlessly
Thanks to the Donald.

"…I grab them by the pussy."
Anatomy, not Trump's strong suit.

"Bigly," Trump's best word,
The beginning and end of Trump positivity.

Our country, our world
Needs help
Very, very bigly.

BRAIN PAIN SONNET

95

Those with right parietal damage to the brain,
Although still alive, have yet to buy the farm.
They neglect, disown, left sided leg or arm,
Yet these patients are not insane.

Last night, May 10, 2023
Trump's CNN Town Hall sycophant fest
MAGA Republicans' political best
8:00 to 9:30, US travesty.

"Undeclared voters" cheered as Trump instructed
People all in for Trump, his deceit and his lies,
Stood, sneered, gave one another high fives.
They did not feel fucked with.

My diagnosis, bad prognosis:
"Right-Side Neglect."

LINDA A.W. BRAKEL, M.D.

THE SUBWAY WAY-1

"Get shot in the Subway," posters advised
As Covid vaccines: needed, not heeded

Poor NYC, so blighted
Rich NYC, wealth and "good taste" in-*breeded.*

    Never the *twain* shall meet.
    On the Subway they do,
    Head on.

THE SUBWAY WAY-2

A man, unhoused and uncared-for, punched
A man, less downtrodden, in the Subway. And
Tore a new body part
Near the heart,
In the Subway.

RUNNING AMOK

What if running amok meant
Running a race? What sort of race would it be?

Or if running a mok meant
Someone sponsored a mok to run in that race?
Of what race(s) would a mok have to be,
To run that race?

Maybe running amok could mean
Running an errand?
What type of errand would an amok be?

What if running a mok meant
Running a tool or piece of equipment?
Example: She ran the delicate mok through the stenosed valve.

But,
Amok derives from the Malay verb "mengamok,"
"To make a furious and desperate charge."

Could running an election be similar to running a mok?

Can a country cry?

LINDA A.W. BRAKEL, M.D.

FLAWS AND ALL; ALL AND ALL
(With Appreciation to Tennison's "Flower in the Crannied Wall")

Congenitally
I am
American.
My Birth Right
My Birth Wrong
I feel guilt
When US
Falters.

Congenitally
My Heart is
Wrong.
Proud, I am
When it Works
Right.
Ashamed
When it
Falters.

People say:
Don't feel guilty
Don't feel ashamed
About your heart
About, this place,
The USA

It isn't you
It's not your fault.

99

Wrong!
I am American
With my Heart
Flaws and All
All and All.

BUY A BIGGER BED

Culture War is
Color War
Red v. Blue
Not
Summer Camp
Competition,
Civil War
No contrition.

****

CRT?
Oh No! White kids
Will feel guilty.
Though when Slavery is not
Addressed
Black kids
FEEL
What?

****

In school libraries
How would it look:
Heather's two Mommies
As a third-grade book?

****

Protect our kids
But not from guns
Nor toxic waste
Nor climate change
Nor folks deranged
Attacking teachers,
School board members,
Doctors helping women choose.

****

Guard the unborn
At all costs--
No maternal care,
Just maternal loss.

****

Once you're born
You're on your own,
But
Don't despair
Don't curse your natural nappy hair.
Soon, yes you can, you really can
Get a gun, your very own!

****

Is there something blue and red,
Some way we can be as one, instead…
A country united in a view,
Something old, nothing new,
Something we all share, not just the few?

****

Yes. Dogs!

Live with a dog
Walk the dog
Brush the dog
Feed the dog
Sleep with the dog.

****

The New York Times
Indeed reports
That red and blue
Do
Unite
In
Sleeping with their dogs.

****

And when the dogs grow bigger,
As some surprisingly do,
What did their people do?
People red and people blue

Bought a bigger bed!

REPLACEMENT THEORY—4 HAIKUS

ECRU JEW
Not pure white, ecru!
I am eggshell, Jew.
No, I will not replace them.

ROT
Don't want to be them.
US: Can you not see them?
Rot in our midst.

MOSQUITOES: QUIET AND CLEVER
Not like mosquitoes,
Numbing the places they bite,
These louts loudly fight.

E PLURIBUS UNUM
E pluribus unum
Great if/when you can get some
Killed by their venom.

HOLDING PATTERN

Hold your horses
Hold your tongue
Though it's slippery and wet.

Hold your fire
Hold the line
Hold your hands up high.
I'm a cop
And you're a black guy
Lest you might forget.

Hold your head up
Hold your ground
Point to bluer sky.

Want to travel,
Want to soar,
Want to someday fly?

Hold your horses
They're so strong.
What we're taught
 Is often wrong.
What we're not,
Ought.